MW01489359

HOW TO WRITE A KPOP FAN MAIL / LETTER IN KOREAN

Ordering Information: Quantity sales. Special discounts are
available on quantity purchases by corporations, associations,
and others. For details, contact the publisher at the email address
above.

Printed in the United States of America

ISBN-13: 979-1188195022

Table of Contents

Why write a fan mail?

▶ You have a crush on a KPOP idol.
▶ You are so deeply moved by their work and want them to know that.
▶ Your life has changed so much (for the better) and you want to express your gratitude.
▶ You want them to know that you exist.
▶ You want them to know that there are people like you who love and care for them.
▶ You think about them 24/7 and just can't get them out of your head.

But whatever the reason is, KPOP idols feed off their fans' love and support. Think about it − whenever they win an award, they always express their gratitude to their fans. They exist because of you. So not only is it to make you feel better, it is actually one of the best ways to keep them motivated and energized. It is something they need the most when they are down, because in reality, they are just like us. Sending them a fan mail full of love and support is like giving them a hug.

Word of advice

► Be polite. They are human beings who deserve respect just like you.
► Don't be too polite or too formal. They want a friend and a supporter who can feel comfortable hanging out with.
► Don't be a creepy stalker. This doesn't need to be explained.
► Don't expect a reply. They get hundreds of fan letters every day.
► But don't assume they all go straight to the trash. They, or someone close to them (e.g., their man-ager or staff members will take the time to read them).
► Don't be afraid of grammatical errors. Even if your Korean is not perfect, it's the thought and effort that count. They are not your Korean language teachers. Even if you make some errors, they can still feel what you are trying to say.

► Do decorate your letters, if you want to.
► Do keep it short and interesting.
► Do use neat handwriting, but bad handwriting is better than a typed letter.
► Do have it proofread. Best if you have a Korean friend around.
► Do check with your local post office to make sure how many stamps to put on the envelope.

How to compose your letter

►Introduce yourself

They want to know you as much as you do. Talk about your name, where your home town is, your age and other fun bits of information such as your blood type and nickname.

►Talk about why you like them so much

This is the part your idol looks forward to reading the most! Show them your love and support.

►Talk about what they mean to you

Do they give you an inspiration? Did they change your life?

►Say thank you

Express your gratitude.

►Closing remarks

Wrap up the letter and include a wish/request if you want.

Labeling the envelope

English Version Sample

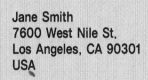

Jane Smith
7600 West Nile St.
Los Angeles, CA 90301
USA

Big Hit Entertainment
Cheonggu Building 2F
13-20, Dosan-daero 16-gil
Gangnam-gu, Seoul 06040
SOUTH KOREA
Attn: 랩 몬스터 (Rap Monster)

Korean Version Sample

Jane Smith
7600 West Nile St.
Los Angeles, CA 90301
USA

서울시 강남구 도산대로 16길 13-20
청구빌딩 2층
빅히트 엔터테인먼트
랩 몬스터 (Rap Monster) 앞
우) 06040
SEOUL, SOUTH KOREA

While both English and Korean versions are acceptable, We'd recommend the Korean version as the Korean post office employees/ mail carriers will find it easier to understand. Make sure, however, that you write SEOUL, SOUTH KOREA in English, so that your country's post office knows where it's going.

*앞 means To/Attn. Add it to the receiver's name (e.g., 씨엘 (CL) 앞)
**우) means postal code (short for 우편번호).

6

Where to send them

JYP Entertainment
(2PM, Wonder Girls, 2AM, miss A, Baek A Yeon, 15&,
SUNMI, GOT7, Bernard Park, G.Soul, DAY6, TWICE, SUZY,
SOMI)

JYP Entertainment
41 Apgujeong-ro 79-gil, Cheongdam-dong,
Gangnam-gu, SEOUL 06012
SOUTH KOREA
Attn: (Your Idol's Name)

서울시 강남구 압구정로 79길 41
JYP 센터
(Your Idol's Name) 앞
우) 06012
SEOUL, SOUTH KOREA

Plan A Entertainment
(Apink, Huh Gak, Jung Eun-ji)

Plan A Entertainment
Star Hill Building 6F, 151, Bongeunsa-ro,
Gangnam-gu, SEOUL 06122
SOUTH KOREA
Attn: (Your Idol's Name)

서울 강남구 봉은사로 151 스타힐빌딩 6층
플랜에이엔터테인먼트
(Your Idol's Name) 앞
우) 06122
SEOUL, SOUTH KOREA

FNC Entertainment

(AOA, CN Blue, FT Island, SF9, N.Fying, Jung Yong Hwa, Lee Hong Gi, JIMIN, INNOVATOR)

FNC Entertainment
46 Dosan-daero 85-gil, Cheongdam-dong, Gangnam-gu, SEOUL 06012
SOUTH KOREA
Attn: (Your Idol's Name)

서울특별시 강남구 도산대로85길 46
FNC 엔터테인먼트
(Your Idol's Name) 앞
우) 06012
SEOUL, SOUTH KOREA

Fantagio Music

(Astro)

Fantagio Music
248, Yeoksam-ro,
Gangnam-gu, SEOUL 06226
SOUTH KOREA
Attn: (Your Idol's Name)

서울특별시 강남구 역삼로 248
판타지오
(Your Idol's Name) 앞
우) 06226
SEOUL, SOUTH KOREA

Big Hit Entertainment
(BTS)

Big Hit Entertainment
Cheonggu Building 2F
13-20, Dosan-daero 16-gil
Gangnam-gu, Seoul 06040
SOUTH KOREA
Attn: (Your Idol's Name)

서울특별시 강남구 도산대로16길 13-20
청구빌딩 2층
빅히트 엔터테인먼트
(Your Idol's Name) 앞
우) 06040
SEOUL, SOUTH KOREA

YG Entertainment
(Big Bang, Black Pink, Psy, Mobb, 2NE1, Winner, iKON,
SechsKies, Epik High, Akdong Musician, Lee Hi, CL)

YG Entertainment
397-5 Hapjeong-dong,
Mapo-gu, SEOUL 04028
SOUTH KOREA
Attn: (Your Idol's Name)

서울특별시 마포구 합정동 397-5
YG 엔터테인먼트
(Your Idol's Name) 앞
우) 04028
SEOUL, SOUTH KOREA

TS Entertainment

(BAP, Secret, Untouchable, Sonamoo, Sleepy, D.Action,
Song Ji Eun, Jun Hyo Seong, Bang & Zelo, Bang Yong Guk)

TS Entertainment
31, Hannam-daero 40-gil,
Yongsan-gu, SEOUL 04417
SOUTH KOREA
Attn: (Your Idol's Name)

서울특별시 용산구 한남대로40길 31
TS 엔터테인먼트
(Your Idol's Name) 앞
우) 04417
SEOUL, SOUTH KOREA

WM Entertainment

(B1A4, Oh My Girl, (I), Sandeul)

WM Entertainment
8, World Cup-ro 15-gil,
Mapo-gu, SEOUL 04012
SOUTH KOREA
Attn: (Your Idol's Name)

서울특별시 마포구 월드컵로15길 8
WM 엔터테인먼트
(Your Idol's Name) 앞
우) 04012
SEOUL, SOUTH KOREA

Around Us Entertainment
(BEAST)

Around Us Entertainment
37-1, Apgujeong-ro 79-gil,
Gangnam-gu, SEOUL 06012
SOUTH KOREA
Attn: (Your Idol's Name)

서울특별시 강남구 청담동 123-45
어라운드 어스 엔터테인먼트
(Your Idol's Name) 앞
우) 06012
SEOUL, SOUTH KOREA

Banana Culture Entertainment
(EXID)

Banana Culture Entertainment
5, Seongsuil-ro 8-gil, Seongdong-gu
Mapo-gu SEOUL 04793
SOUTH KOREA
Attn: (Your Idol's Name)

서울특별시 성동구 성수일로8길 5
서울숲 SK V1타워 B동 지하 1층
바나나컬쳐 엔터테인먼트
(Your Idol's Name) 앞
우) 04793
SEOUL, SOUTH KOREA

KQ Entertainment
(Block B)

KQ Entertainment
Jay Studio 3F
28, Donggyo-ro 25-gil,
Mapo-gu, SEOUL 03993
SOUTH KOREA
Attn: (Your Idol's Name)

서울특별시 마포구 동교로 25길 28,
제이스튜디오 3층
KQ 엔터테인먼트
(Your Idol's Name) 앞
우) 03993
SEOUL, SOUTH KOREA

Cube Entertainment
(BtoB, Hyuna, Jang Hyun Seung, CLC, Trouble Maker, Roh
Jihoon, Pentagon, Kim Kiri, Na Jongchan)

Cube Entertainment
F2 Building
83 Achasan-ro,
Seongdong-gu, Seoul SEOUL 04793
SOUTH KOREA
Attn: (Your Idol's Name)

서울특별시 성동구 아차산로 83
F2빌딩
큐브 엔터테인먼트
(Your Idol's Name) 앞
우) 04793
SEOUL, SOUTH KOREA

SM Entertainment
(EXO, TBXQ, TRAX, Super Junior, Girls' Generation, SHINee, f(x), Red Velvet, NCT, BoA, ZhangLiYin)

SM Entertainment
648, Samseong-ro, Gangnam-gu
Gangnam-gu, SEOUL 06084
SOUTH KOREA
Attn: (Your Idol's Name)

서울특별시 강남구 삼성로 648
SM 엔터테인먼트
(Your Idol's Name) 앞
우) 06084
SEOUL, SOUTH KOREA

Woollim Entertainment
(Jang Jun & Young Taek, Joo Chan & So Yoon, INFINITE)

Woollim Entertainment
14, World Cup buk-ro 23-gil,
Mapo-gu, SEOUL 03966
SOUTH KOREA
Attn: (Your Idol's Name)

서울특별시 마포구 월드컵북로 23길 14
울림 엔터테인먼트
(Your Idol's Name) 앞
우) 03966
SEOUL, SOUTH KOREA

RBW Entertainment

(MAMAMOO, VROMANCE, Basick, Yangpa, Monday Kiz, O Broject, eSNa, Big Tray)

RBW Entertainment
7, Janghan-Ro, 20-Gil,
Dongdaemun-Gu, SEOUL 02639
SOUTH KOREA
Attn: (Your Idol's Name)

서울특별시 동대문구 장한로20길 7
RBW 엔터테인먼트
(Your Idol's Name) 앞
우) 02639
SEOUL, SOUTH KOREA

NH MEDIA

(Lim Chang Jung, U-KISS, LABOUM, The Ray, SOUL LATIDO)

NH MEDIA
10-23 Nonhyeon 1-dong,
Mapo-gu, SEOUL 06040
SOUTH KOREA
Attn: (Your Idol's Name)

서울특별시 강남구 논현1동 10-23
NH 미디어
(Your Idol's Name) 앞
우) 06040
SEOUL, SOUTH KOREA

TOP MEDIA
(ANDY, TEENTOP, 100%, PARK Dong Min, UP10TION)

TOP Media
47, Bongeunsa-ro 55-gil,
Gangnam-gu, SEOUL 06093
SOUTH KOREA
Attn: (Your Idol's Name)

서울특별시 강남구 봉은사로55길 47
티오피 미디어
(Your Idol's Name) 앞
우) 06093
SEOUL, SOUTH KOREA

Starship Entertainment
(K.WILL, Sistar, Boyfriend, Mad Clown, Jung Gi Go,
MONSTA X, BrotherSu, WJSN, #GUN)

Starship Entertainment
Starhill Building 4F
151, Bongeunsa-ro,
Gangnam-gu, SEOUL 06122
SOUTH KOREA
Attn: (Your Idol's Name)

서울특별시 강남구 봉은사로 151
스타빌딩 4층
스타쉽엔터테인먼트
(Your Idol's Name) 앞
우) 06122
SEOUL, SOUTH KOREA

Star Empire Entertainment
(Nine Muses, ZE:A, Seo In Young, Impact)

Star Empire Entertainment
48, Seongji-gil,
Mapo-gu, SEOUL 04083
SOUTH KOREA
Attn: (Your Idol's Name)

서울특별시 마포구 성지길 48
스타제국
(Your Idol's Name) 앞
우) 04083
SEOUL, SOUTH KOREA

Fan Mail
Expressions

How to Use The Expressions

The expressions are customizable, meaning that you can create your own sentence by inserting the words you want. Those fields are presented in parenthesis so you know exactly what goes where. Simply pick, customize, and combine the expressions of your choice and you just wrote a KPOP fan letter in Korean that sounds 100% natural!

Some useful tips:

▶ How to address your idol

Some of the most commonly used ones are:

〉오빠 – If you are a younger female addressing an older male idol.
Example) GD 오빠, 안녕하세요?

〉형 – If you are a younger male addressing an older male idol.
Example) Tony 형, 안녕하세요?

〉누나 – If you are a younger male addressing an older female idol.
Example)
BoA 누나, 만나서 반가워요!

> 언니 – If you are a younger female addressing an older female idol.
Example) Jenny 언니, 정말 예뻐요!

> 당신 – If you want to address someone you don't know in a formal way. It is used on its own.

Example) 당신은 정말 멋있어요!

> ~씨 – If you want to address someone you don't know in a formal way using the name.

Example) GD씨, 안녕하세요?

> ~야 – If you want to be extra friendly. It is used between friends of same age, to someone younger.

Example) Tony야, 안녕?

► How to choose the proper direct object particle "을/를"

> If your word ends with a vowel (ㅏ / ㅑ / ㅓ / ㅕ / ㅗ / ㅛ / ㅜ / ㅠ / ㅡ / ㅣ / ㅒ / ㅖ / ㅘ / ㅙ / ㅝ / ㅞ / ㅚ / ㅟ / ㅢ), use "를"

Example) 소미 (Somi) 를, 오빠 (oppa) 를, 나 (na) 를

> If your word ends with a consonant, use "을"

*It's not the English spelling that matters. The rule applies to how the Korean word ends. For example, while 컴퓨터 (computer) is spelled to end with a consonant in English, the Korean word ends with a vowel "ㅓ". Hence you use "를"

Example) 빅뱅 (Big Bang) 을, 지드래곤 (G-Dragon) 을, SM 타운 (SM Town) 을

► How to choose the proper topic particle "는/은"

〉 If your word ends with a vowel, use "는"
Example) 바나나 (banana) 는, 오빠 (oppa) 는, 블랙핑크 (Black Pink) 는

*Again, while Black Pink ends with a consonant in English, it ends with a vowel
"ㅡ" in Korean. Hence you use "는"

〉 If your words ends with a consonant, use "은"

Example) 빅뱅 (Big Bang) 은, 지드래곤 (G-Dragon) 은, 레드벨벳 (Red Velvet) 은.

► How to choose the proper subject particle "이/가"

〉 If your word ends with a vowel, use "가"
Example) GD 오빠 (GD oppa) 가, 아이유 언니 (IU unnie) 가

> If your words ends with a consonant, use "이"

Example) 빅뱅 (Big Bang) 이, 레드벨벳 (Red Velvet) 이.

▶ **Use an online Korean dictionary to find the words you need.**

Whenever you come across a customizable blank, use any of the following to find the Korean word for it.

Google translator – translate.google.com (best for Western languages (English, Spanish, French, and etc.)

Naver translator – translate.naver.com (best for Asian languages (Chinese, Japanese, Thai, Indonesian, Vietnamese, and etc.)

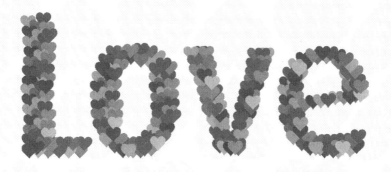

Greetings & Introduction

1. (   ) 에게,
To/Dear (   ),

2. 사랑하는 (   ) 에게,
To my dearest (   ),

3. 안녕?
Hello/Hi (informal, between friends)

4. 안녕하세요?
Hello/Hi/How are you? (formal)

5. 잘 지냈어요?
How have you been?
(literal meaning : Have you been well?)

6. 어떻게 지냈어요?
How have you been?

7. 그동안 별 일 없었어요?
Anything new down your way?

8. 정말 오랜만이에요!
It really has been a long time!

9. 오랜만에 편지를 써요.
It's been a while since I wrote to you.

10. (만나서/알게되어서) 기뻐요.
It's a pleasure (meeting/knowing) you.

11. 처음으로 (   ) 에게 편지를 써요.
This is my first time writing a letter to you.

12. 제 이름은 (   ) 이에요.
My name is (   ).

13. 저는 (   ) 이에요.
I am (a) (   ).

Example) 학생 – student, 멕시코 사람 – Mexican,
중국 사람 – Chinese, 필리핀 사람 – Filipino
프랑스 사람 – French 영국 사람 – English
(British)

14. 제 혈액형은 (   ) 이에요.
My blood type is (   ).

15. 저는 (   ) 에 살아요.
I live in (   ).

16. 한국어 잘 못해요.
My Korean isn't very good. / My Korean is poor.

17. 한국어 공부하고 있어요.
I am studying Korean.

18. 한국어 잘 못해서 미안해요.
I am sorry my Korean isn't good.

19. 한국어 잘 못하지만 이해해 주세요.
Please excuse my bad (poor) Korean.

20. 친구가 도와주고 있어요.
My friend is helping me out.

21. 친구도 (   ) 팬이에요.
My friend is also a fan of (   ).

22. 혼자서 한국어로 편지 쓰고 싶어요.
I want to write a letter in Korean by myself.

23. 한국어 잘하고 싶어요.
I want to be good at Korean.

24. 한국어 공부 열심히해서 (   ) 에게 제 마음을 전하고 싶어요.
I want to study Korean hard so I can express my feelings to (   ).

25. 한국어 공부는 정말 어려워요.
Studying Korean is very difficult.

26. 하지만 최선을 다할거에요.
But I will do my very best.

27. (   ) 에게 하고 싶은 이야기가 많아요.
I have so many things to share with you/tell you.

28. 저는 (   ) 에 살아요.
I live in (   ).

29. 저는 (   ) 살 이에요.
I am (   ) years old.

30. 제 별명은 (   ) 이에요.
People call me / My nickname is (   ).

31. 저는 (엄마/아빠/강아지) 와 함께 살아요.
I live with (mom/dad/puppy).

32. 저는 (   ) 에서 태어났어요.
I was born in (   ).

33. 저는 (   ) 출신이에요.
I am from / I come from (   ).

34. 이곳은 (   ) 마을 / 도시 에요.
It is a (   ) village / city.

35. 이곳은 (   ) 로 유명해요.
It is famous for (   ).

36. 저는 (   ) 에게 편지 쓰려고 한국어를
공부해요.
I study Korean so I can write a letter to you.

37. 저는 (   )* 를(을) (   )** 동안
좋아했어요.
I have been a fan of (   )* for (   )**.
/ I've loved (   )* since (   )**.

38. 한국에 가보고 싶어요.
I want to visit Korea.

39. 우리 (   ) 때 (   ) 에서 만났어요.
We've met at a (   ) in/at (   ).

26

40. 우리는 만난적은 없어요.
We've never met.

41. (　　　　) 생각만 하면 웃음이 나와요.
Just thinking about you makes me smile.

42. (　　　　) 는(은) 나를 웃게 만들어요.
(　　　　) make(s) me smile.

43. (　　　　) 의 노래/목소리를 들으면 눈물이
나요.
I cry when I hear/listen to (　　　　) song/voice.

44. (　　　) 의 노래/목소리를 들으면 에너지가
생겨요.
I become full of energy when I hear/listen to
(　　　　) song/voice.

45. (　　　) 의 얼굴/video를 보면 눈물이 나요.
I cry when I see (　　　　) face/video.

46. (　　　　) 의 얼굴/video를 보면 에너지가
생겨요.
I become full of energy when I see (　　　　)
face/video.

27

47. (   ) 가(이) 나와 같은 하늘 아래에 살고
있다는 사실에 기분이 너무좋아요.
The fact that (   ) and I live under the
same sky (in the same world) makes me feel so
happy.

48. (   ) 는(은) (   ) 를(을) 좋아해요?
Do(es) (   ) like (   )?

49. (콘서트/사인회/시사회/TV쇼/영화)**에서
(   )* 를 보았어요.
I saw (   )* at/in (concert/fan signing/
movie screening/TV show/movie)**.

50. 데뷔때부터 팬이었어요.
I've been a fan since debut.

51. 당신과 같은 사람은 이 세상에 없어요.
There is no one like you in the world.

52. (   ) 를(을) 본 순간부터 사랑에 빠졌어요.
I fell in love from the moment I saw (   ).

53. (오빠)* (목소리/노래)** 를(을) 들은 순간부터
사랑에 빠졌어요.
I fell in love from the moment I heard
(oppa=your)* (voice/song)**.

28

54. (   ) 는(은) 정말 (예뻐/멋있어/잘생겼어/
아름다워/사랑스러워/똑똑해/재밌어)*요.
(   ) is/are so (pretty/cool/handsome/
beautiful/lovely/smart/funny)*.

55. (   ) 는(은) 세상에서 가장 (예뻐/
멋있어/잘생겼어/아름다워/사랑스러워/
똑똑해/재밌어)요.
(   ) is/are the prettiest/coolest/most
handsome/most beautiful/loveliest/smartest/
funniest

56. (   ) 는(은) 친절한 사람이에요.
(   ) is/are a kind person.

57. (   ) 의 건강과 행복을 위해 기도해요.
I pray for your health and happiness.

58. (   ) 가(이) 아프면 나도 아파요.
When (   ) is/are sick (hurt), I feel sick
(hurt) too.

59. (   ) 가(이) 슬프면 나도 슬퍼요.
When (   ) is/are sad, I feel sad too.

60. (   ) 가(이) 행복하면 나도 행복해요.

If (   ) is/are happy, I feel happy too.
61. (   ) 는(은) (노래/댄스/연기/공부/기타연주/공연)* 할때 가장 (예뻐/멋있어/잘생겼어/아름다워/사랑스러워/재밌어)**요.
(   ) is/are/look the (prettiest/coolest/most handsome/most beautiful/loveliest/funniest)** when (singing/dancing/acting/studying/playing the guitar/performing)*.

62. (   ) 는(은) 저에게 큰 영감이에요.
(   ) is/are a huge inspiration to me.

63. (   ) 의 콘서트에 갈거에요.
I am going to (   ) concert.

64. (   )의 콘서트에 갔었어요.
I went to (   ) concert.

65. 매일 (   ) 의 노래를 들어요.
I listen to (   ) song everyday.

66. >매일 (   ) 가 나오는 영상을 봐요.
I watch (   ) video clips everyday.

67. (   ) 의 콘서트에 가는게 제 소원이에요.
I really wish to go to (   ) concert.

68. 항상 보고싶어요.
I always miss you.

69. 항상 (   ) 생각해요.
I always think about you.

70. 자나깨나 (   ) 생각해요.
I think about (   ) 24/7
71. 가슴이 너무 뛰어요.
My heart is pounding so fast.

72. 정말 정말 행복해요.
I am really really happy.

~ Useful Words ~

73. 최근에 (recently)

74. 마지막으로 (lastly)

75. 처음으로 (for the first time)

76. 다시 한번 (one more time)

77. 진짜로 (really)

78. 솔직히 (honestly / frankly)
79. 솔직히 말해서 (frankly speaking)

80. 진심으로 (wholeheartedly)

81. 언제나 (always)

82. 매일 (everyday)

Expressing Gratitude

83. 고마워요.
Thank you.

84. 감사합니다.
I appreciate it.

85. 언제나 훌륭한 (노래/영화/드라마/music video)에 감사하고 있어요.
I am always grateful for your outstanding (song/movie/drama/music video).

86. 팬들을 생각해줘서 고마워요.
Thank you for thinking of your fans.

87. (   )없는 세상은 상상하기 싫어요.
I don't want to imagine a world without (   ).

88. 모든 팬들이 고마워해요.
All of the fans are thankful for it.

89. (   ) 덕분에 많은것이 바뀌었어요.
Because of (   ), lots of things have changed.

90. 물론, 좋은 쪽으로요.
For the better, of course.

91. 희망을 주어서 고마워요.
Thank you for giving me a hope.

92. 여러가지로 고마워요.
Thank you for everything.

93. 덕분에 매일 행복해요.
Thanks to you, I am happy everyday.

94. 고마움으로 가득해요.
I am full of gratitude.

95. 언제나 고맙다고 말하고 싶었어요.
I've always wanted to say thank you.

96. 부끄러움을 좀 타지만, 고마워요.
I am a little shy to say this, but thank you.

97. 고맙다는 표현을 어떻게 해야 충분한지 모르겠어요.
I don't know how to thank you enough.

98. 많이 고맙다는 뜻이에요.

That means I am really thankful for it.
99. 고마움에 보답할게요.
I will repay you for your kindness.

100. (   )는(은) 정말 친절한 사람이에요.
(   ) is/are a really kind person.

101. (   )는(은) 정말 친절하고 상냥해요.
(   ) is/are really kind and friendly.

102. (   ) 덕분에 웃어요.
I smile because of (   ).

103. (   )는(은) 나의 기쁨이에요.
(   ) is/are my pleasure.

104. 세상에 와줘서 고마워요.
Thank you for coming to this world.

105. 얼마나 고마운지 몰라요!
You don't even know how thankful I am!

106. 진심으로 감사합니다.
I sincerely appreciate it.

107. 깊이 감사드리고 있어요.
I'm deeply grateful to you.

108. 어쨌든 정말 고마워요.
Thank you so much anyway.

109. 도와줘서 고마워요.
Thank you for helping me.

110. 기다려줘서 고마워요.
Thank you for waiting.

111. 걱정해줘서 고마워요.
Thank you for your concern.

112. 작지만 감사의 표시에요.
This is a small token of appreciation.

113. 우리는 매우 감사하고 고마워하고 있어요.
We are very appreciative end very grateful.

114. 다시 한번 (   )의 노고에 감사드려요.
Thank you again for (   ) hard work.

115. 시간 내주셔서 고마워요.
Thank you for your time.

116. 바쁘실텐데 제 편지 읽어주셔서 고마워요.
Thank you for taking the time out of your busy

schedule to read my letter.

117. 친절을 베풀어주셔서 깊이 감사드려요.
I thank you from the bottom of my heart for
your kindness.

118. 뭐라고 감사해야 할 지 모르겠어요.
I have no words to express my gratitude.

119. 저에게 영감을 주셔서 고마워요.
Thank you for being my inspiration.

120. 저에게 큰 힘이 되어주셔서 고마워요.
Thank you for being a great encouragement.

121. 그렇게 말해주니 고마워요,
It's kind of you to say that.

122. 어떻게 보답해야 할까요?
How can I ever repay you?

123. 큰 힘이 되어주었어요.
You've been a great help.

124. (   ) 에게 고맙다고 전해주세요.
Please give my thanks to (   ).

125. 정말 행복해요.

I am really happy.
126. 행복하게 만들어줘서 고마워요.
Thank you for making me happy.

127. 매일 행복해요.
I am happy everyday.

128. 이렇게 행복했던 적은 없어요.
I've never been this happy.

129. 밥을 안먹어도 배가 불러요.
I feel full without eating = (I'm happy 24/7).

130. 행복이란 이런 느낌인가봐요.
This must be what happiness feels like.

131. 행복/사랑 이라는 것을 알게 해주었어요.
You taught me what happiness/love feels like.

132. 항상 고마워 하며 살게요.
I will always be thankful to you.

133. (   )에 와주셔서 고마워요!
Thanks for coming to (   )!

134. (   )에서 콘서트를 해주셔서 고마워요!
Thanks for having a concert in/at (   )!

135. 훌륭한 롤모델이 되어줘서 고마워요!
Thanks for being a great role model!

136. 언제나 웃음을 잃지 않아줘서 고마워요!
Thank you for always having a smile on your face!

137. 최고가 되어줘서 고마워요.
Thank you for being the best.

138. 이 세상에 단 하나뿐인 존재가 되어줘서 고마워요.
Thank you for being the one and only.

139. (저를/우리를)잊지 않아줘서 고마워요.
Thank you for not forgetting (me/us).

140. (저를/우리를) 특별하게 만들어 줘서 고마워요.
Thank you for making (me/us) feel special.

~ Useful Words ~

141. 항상 (always)

Example) 항상 보고싶어요. (I always miss you.)

142. ~에서 (at/in/on)
Example) 콘서트에서 (at a concert) 무대에서 (on the stage)

143. 이 세상에 (in this world)
144. ~에게 (to)
Example) 오빠에게 (to oppa)

145. ~덕분에 (thanks to)
Example) 오빠 덕분에 (thanks to oppa)

146. 웃어요 (I smile)

147. 행복해요 (I am happy)

Congratulatory Messages

148. 축하해요!
Congratulations!

149. 축하합니다!
Congratulations (formal).

150. 생일 축하합니다!
Happy Birthday! (literal meaning = I congratulate your birthday)

151. (대상/본상) 타신것 축하해요!
Congratulations on winning the daesang/ bonsang!

152. 상 타실 것 알고있었어요.
I knew you'd win that award.

153. 새 앨범 나온 것 축하해요!
Congratulations on your new album release!

154. (드라마/영화/TV쇼)에 캐스팅 되신 것 축하해요!
Congratulations on getting a role in the (drama/

movie/TV show).

155. (   ) 주년을 축하해요!
Happy (   ) anniversary!

156. 데뷔 (   ) 주년을 축하해요!
Happy (   ) debut anniversary!

157. 1등을 축하해요!
Congratulations on being #!

158. 차트 1등을 축하해요!
Congratulations on topping the chart!

159. 차트 올킬을 축하해요!
Congratulations on "all-killing" the charts!

160. 트리플 크라운을 축하해요!
Congratulations on achieving "Triple Crown"!

161. 새로 나온 (뮤직비디오/노래) 정말 멋져요!
The newly released (music video/song) is really awesome!

162. 새 (헤어 스타일/패션) 정말 멋져요!
Your new (hair style/fashion) is so cool!

163. 새 앨범에 있는 곡들 전부 다 좋아요!

I like every single song in the new album.

164. 새 (컨셉/CF/안무) 정말 (멋져요/섹시해요/
신비해요).
The new (concept/CF/choreograph) is really
(cool/sexy/mysterious).

165. 진심으로 축하해요!
I extend to you my heartiest congratulations!

166. 새 멤버가 생긴걸 축하해요!
Congratulations on the new addition to the
group! (= new member to the group)

167. 그럴 자격이 있어요!
You deserve it! / You earned it!

168. 해냈어요!
You did it! / You made it!

169. 계속 잘 해주세요!
Keep up the good work!

~ Useful Words ~

170. 새 (new) + noun
Example) 새 신발 (new shoes)

171. 새로 나온 (newly released) + noun
Example) 새로 나온 영화 (newly released movie)

172. Noun + 좋아요 (I like ~sth) : Example)
강아지 좋아요 (I like puppies)

173. ~(number) 주년 (~th anniversary) :
Example) 주년 (th year anniversary)

174. 생일 (birthday) / 상 (award) / 1등 (1st place)

175. 노래 (song)

Compliments

176. (   ) 팬들이 정말 많아요.
(   ) have so many fans here.

177. 팬클럽 회원이 정말 많아요.
The fan club has so many members.

178. 모두 (   ) 의 팬이에요.
We are all fans of (   ).

179. (   ) 은/는 춤을 정말 잘춰요.
(   ) is/are such a great dancer.

180. (연기/노래)를 어떻게 그렇게 잘해요?
How can you be so good at (acting/singing)?

181. 어떻게 그렇게 (예뻐요/멋져요/잘생겼어요/
웃겨요/재밌어요)?
How can you be so (pretty/cool/handsome/
hilarious/funny)?

182. 왜 그렇게 (예뻐요/멋져요/잘생겼어요/
웃겨요/재밌어요)?
Why are you so (pretty/cool/handsome/

45

hilarious/funny)?

183. 언제부터 그렇게 (예뻤어요/멋졌어요/
잘생겼었어요/웃겼어요/재밌었어요)?
Since when have you been so (pretty/cool/
handsome/hilarious/funny)?

184. 매력이 넘쳐요.
You are very charming.

185. 매력 덩어리에요.
You are full of charm = You are my McDreamy.

186. 최고에요.
You are the best.

187. 최고중의 최고에요.
You are the best of the best.

188. (   )를/을 제일 좋아해요.
I like (   ) the most.

189. (   ) 는(은) 정말 특별해요.
(   ) is/are so special.

190. (   ) 는(은) 세상에 단 하나밖에 없는
사람이에요.

(   ) is/are the one and only person in the world.

191. (   ) 는(은) 하늘이 주신 선물이에요.
(   ) is/are a gift from heaven.

192. (   ) 는(은) 내 인생에 가장 큰 선물이에요.
(   ) is/are the greatest gift/present of my life.

193. (   ) 는(은) 내 인생의 큰 의미에요.
(   ) mean(s) a lot in my life.

194. (   ) 없는 세상은 너무 외롭고 슬플 것 같아요.
The world without (   ) will be so lonely and sad.

195. (   ) 는(은) 천사같아요.
(   ) is/are like an angel.

196. (   ) 는(은) 나에게 모든것이에요.
(   ) mean(s) everything to me.

197. 목소리가 정말 달콤해요/섹시해요.
Your voice is so sweet/sexy.

198. 모두에게 친절해서 좋아요.

47

I like the fact that you are kind to everyone.

199. 똑똑하고 친절해요.
You are smart and kind.

200. 정말 완벽해요.
You are really perfect.

201. 완벽 그 자체에요.
You are perfection itself.

202. 모든걸 다 가진 사람이에요.
You are a man who has everything.

203. 저도 (   ) 처럼 되고 싶어요.
I want to be like (   ).

204. (   ) 이/가 정말 (예뻐요/멋져요/섹시해요).
Your (   ) is/are so pretty/cool/sexy.

205. 유머 감각이 뛰어나세요.
You have a great sense of humor.

206. 몸매가 정말 좋으세요.
You are in such great shape.

207. (   )를/을 닮으셨어요.
You look like (   ).

208. (   )* 를 보면 (   )** 생각이나요.
(   )* remind me of (   )**.

209. 어떻게 몸매를 유지해요?
How do you stay in shape?

210. 훌륭한 남편이 될거에요.
You will make a great husband.

211. 훌륭한 아내가 될거에요.
You will make a great wife.

212. 당당함이 멋져요.
I admire your confidence.

213. 타고난 리더에요.
You are a natural-born leader.

214. 모두들 당신을 존경해요.
Everyone looks up to you.

215. 우리 모두의 우상이에요.
You are our idol.

216. 우리는 (   )을 숭배해요!
We worship (   ).

217. (   ) 는/은 우리의 수호천사에요.
(   ) is/are our guardian angel.

218. (   ) 이/가 함께 있다고 생각하면 마음이 든든해요.
I feel safe when I think (   ) is/are with me.

219. 존재만으로도 힘이되요.
Your mere existence is a great support.

220. (   )의 노래를 들으면 힘이 솟아요!
Listening to (   ) song gives me energy!

221. (   ) 는/은 눈부신 빛과 같아요.
(   ) is/are like a bright light.
222. (   ) 는/은 태양과 같이 밝아요.
(   ) is/are bright like the sun.

223. 내 인생의 태양.
The sun of my life.

224. 내 인생의 (의미/목적).
The meaning/purpose of my life.

225. 내가 아침에 눈을 뜨는 이유.
The reason I open my eyes in the morning.

226. 내가 살아가는 이유.
The reason I live.

227. 그게 바로 (   )입니다.
That is because of (   ).

228. 나도 (   )에게 힘이 되고 싶어요.
I also want to be your support.

~ Useful Words ~

229. 우리는 (we are)
Example) 우리는 행복해요. We are happy.

230. 나도 (I also, me too)
Example) 나도 행복해요. I am also happy.

231. 어떻게 (how)
232. 왜 (why)

233. ~같아요 (look/feel/sound like ~ sth)
Example) 강아지 같아요. You (look) like a puppy.

Showing Support

234. 화이팅!
Fighting (= cheer up! / let's go!)

235. 힘내요!
Cheer up!

236. 잘 될 거에요!
It's going to be all right!

237. 성공할거에요!
It will be a success!

238. 대박을 기원합니다.
Hope you win it big! (= wishing you the best of luck!)

239. 성공은 따놓은 당상이에요.
There is no doubt it will be a success.

240. 잘 했어요!
Way to go!

241. 짱이에요! (= informal 최고에요!)
You are the best!

242. 믿을 수가 없어요!
Unbelievable!

243. 생각보다 훨씬 (멋져요/예뻐요/섹시해요/ 잘생겼어요/좋아요)
It's cooler/prettier/sexier/more handsome/ better than I've imagined.

244. 언제나 응원합니다.
I'm always on your side.

245. 언제나 응원하는거 알죠?
You know I'm always on your side, right?

246. 우리가 있잖아요!
We are here for you!

247. 걱정할 필요 없어요.
There is no need to worry.

248. 걱정마세요.
Don't worry about it.

249. 하나도 걱정하지 마세요.
Don't you worry about a thing.

250. 성공은 당연해요.
Your success is guaranteed.

251. 우리가 서포트해요.
We will be there to support.

252. (   ) 를(을) 사랑하는 팬들이 정말 많아요.
There are many fans who love (   ).

253. (저/우리)가 (   )에 응원하러 갈거에요.
I/We will be at (   ) to support you.

254. 큰 소리로 외칠거에요.
I will cry at the top of my voice.

255. 함께 노래 할거에요.
I will sing along with you.

256. 형광봉을 흔들거에요.
I will be waving a light stick.

257. 정말 환상적일거에요.
It will be really fantastic.

258. 꿈꿔왔던 순간이 될거에요.
It will be a dream-come-true moment.

259. 실수해도 괜찮아요.
It's okay if you make a mistake.

260. 어떻게 해도 사랑스러워요.
You are lovely, no matter what.

261. 행동 하나 하나가 사랑스러워요.
Every single move you make is lovely.

262. 실패해도 괜찮아요.
It's okay if you fail.

263. 다음에 더 잘할거에요.
You will do better next time.

264. 제 느낌은 틀린적이 없어요.
My feelings have never been wrong.

265. 좋은 느낌이 들어요.
I have a good feeling about it.

266. 끝내줬어요!
That was awesome! (informal = That was the bomb!)

267. 힘들땐 (제/우리) 생각을 해주세요.
Please think about me/us whenever you are feeling down.

268. 항상 기도할거에요.
I will always be praying for you.

269. 본방사수 할거에요!
I will watch it live!

270. 대상 타기를 기원할게요!
I wish you win the grand prize!

271. 반드시 1등 할거에요!
I am sure you will win the first place!

272. 울지 말아요!
Please don't cry!

273. 안타깝지만, 슬퍼하지 말아요.
It is a pity (= it is a shame), but don't feel sad.

274. 다음이 있잖아요!
There is always next time!

275. 엄청난 신인이에요!
You are an amazing rookie!

276. (　　　　) 의 뉴스를 보았어요.
I saw the news about (　　　　).

277. (　　　　)의 이야기를 들었어요.
I heard the story about (　　　　).

278. 저는 언제나 (　　　　) 를(을) 믿어요.
I always trust (　　　　).

279. 그런 소문따위 믿지 않아요.
I don't believe the rumors.

280. (　　　　)만 믿어요.
I only believe in (　　　　).

281. 누가 뭐라고 하던지.
No matter what they say.

282. 다른사람들이 하는 말 신경쓰지 마세요.
Don't worry about what others say.

283. 다른사람들이 하는 생각 신경쓰지 마세요.
Don't worry about what other people think.

284. 그냥 하는 일에만 집중하세요.
Just focus on what you are doing.

285. 그게 (제가/우리가) 원하는 것이에요.
That's what I/we want.

286. 제 편지를 보고 힘내세요!
I hope my letter cheers you up!

287. 좋은 생각과 기운을 보냅니다.
Sending good thoughts and vibes.

288. 저는 (   ) 가(이) 정말 자랑스러워요.
I am really proud of (   ).

289. (   ) 는(은) 제 인생을 바꾸었어요.
(   ) changed my life.

290. (   ) 덕분에 힘든 시간을 버텨낼 수 있었어요.
Thanks to (   ), I was able to persevere through the hard times.

291. (   ) 는(은) 제 은인이에요!
(   ) is/are the savior of my life! / I am very indebted to (   ).

~ Useful Words ~

292. 믿어요 (I believe)

293. 힘내세요! (cheer up!)

294. 하나도 (not even a thing, not at all)
Example) 하나도 안 무서워요 not afraid at all

295. 알죠? You know, right?

Expressing Concerns

296. 아프지 말아요.
Don't get sick.

297. 많이 아프다고 들었어요.
I heard you are very sick.

298. 마음이 많이 아프겠어요.
You must be heartbroken.

299. 많이 슬프겠어요.
You must be very sad.

300. 우울해하지 말아요.
Don't be so depressed.

301. 많이 다쳤어요?
Are you badly hurt?

302. 많이 다치지 않았으면 좋겠어요.
I hope you are not too hurt.

303. 많이 슬퍼하지 않았으면 좋겠어요.
I hope you don't feel too bad.

304. 빨리 나으세요.
I hope you get better soon.

305. 우리 모두 걱정하고 있어요.
We are all worried.

306. 너무 걱정되요.
I'm so worried.

307. (   )에 대해서 너무 걱정이 되요.
I am so worried about (   ).

308. 걱정하게 만들지 말아주세요.
Please don't make me worry.

309. 실망 많이 했죠?
You must have been so disappointed.

310. 많이 힘들었죠?
You must have suffered a lot.

311. 얼마나 힘들었을까.
I can't imagine how difficult it must have been.

312. 모두 다 괜찮아 질거에요.
Everything will be all right.

313. 힘들때는 좀 쉬어요.
Try to take a break when you feel exhausted.

314. 완벽한 사람은 없어요.
Nobody's perfect.

315. 물론, (   )은/는 완벽에 가장 가까운 사람이지만요.
Of course, you are the closest thing to perfection.

316. 너무 열심히 일하지 마세요.
Don't work too hard.

317. 안티는 무시하세요.
Just ignore anti fans.

318. 부러워서 그러는거에요.
They act like that because they are jealous.

319. 괜찮을 것 같아요?
You think you will be okay?

320. 괜찮을 거라고 생각해요.
I think you will be all right.

321. 울지 말아요!
Don't cry.

322. 너무 기쁠때만 울어요!
Cry only when you are too happy!

323. 어떻게 하면 (제/우리)가 도움이 될 수 있을까요?
How can I/we be of help?

324. 건강이 가장 중요해요.
Health is the most important thing.

325. 밥 잘 챙겨 먹어요.
Don't skip meals.

326. 술 너무 많이 마시지 마세요.
Don't drink too much.

327. 파티 너무 많이 하지 마세요.
Don't party too hard.

328. 몸에 좋은 것 많이 먹어요.
Eat lots of things that are good for your body.

329. 잠 많이 자요.
Sleep a lot.

330. 운전 조심해요.
Drive carefully.

331. 음주운전은 절대 안되요!
Drunk driving is never okay!

332. 문자 하면서 (운전하지/걸어가지) 말아요.
Don't text while driving/walking on the street.

333. (   )의 행복이 (저/우리)의 행복이에요!
Your happiness is my/our happiness!

334. 싸우지 말아요.
Don't fight

335. 멤버들끼리 사이좋게 지내세요.
Please get along with your members.

336. 서로 조금씩 양보해요.
Each should give in a little.

337. (제/우리) 걱정은 하지 마세요.
Don't worry about me/us.

~ Useful Words ~

338. 완벽한 (perfect)

339. 걱정 (worry)

340. 양보 (yield/to give in)

341. 안티 (anti fans)

342. 물론 (of course)

Wishes & Requests

343. (   ) 에 꼭 와주세요!
I really hope that you would visit us in (   ).

344. (   ) 에 다시 와주기를 기원할게요!
I wish you to come back to visit us in (   )!

345. 하지만 꼭 만나고 싶어요.
But I really want to meet you.

346. 언젠가는 만날거라고 믿어요.
I believe we will meet sometime.

347. 언젠가는 꿈이 꼭 이루어 질거라고 믿어요.
I believe that dreams will come true one day.

348. (   ) 를(을) 만나게 되면 세상에서 가장 행복할 것 같아요.
I think I will be the happiest person in the world if I met (   ).

349. (   ) 를(을) 만나게 되면 너무 좋아서 눈물이 날 것 같아요.
I think I will cry tears of joy if I meet (   ).

350. (   ) 의 손을 잡고 싶어요.
I want to hold (   ) hand.

351. (   ) 와 함께 걷고 싶어요.
I want to walk with (   ).

352. (   ) 와 함께 노래부르고 싶어요.
I want to sing with (   ).

353. (   ) 와 함께 영화보고 싶어요.
I want to go to the movies with (   ).

354. (   ) 와 함께 사진찍고 싶어요.
I want to take a picture with (   ).

355. (   ) 와 함께 여행하고 싶어요.
I want to travel with (   ).

356. (   ) 와 함께 데이트하고 싶어요.
I want to go on a date with (   ).

357. (   ) 와 결혼하고 싶어요.
I want to marry (   ).

358. (   ) 의 여자친구가 되고 싶어요.
I want to be (   ) girlfriend.

359. (　　　) 의 남자친구가 되고 싶어요.
I want to be (　　　) boyfriend.

360. (　　　) 가(이) 항상 제 곁에 있어주었으면 좋겠어요.
I always want to have you right here by my side.

361. 실물로 만나보고 싶어요.
I want to meet you in the flesh.

362. 라이브로 보고 싶어요.
I want to see it live.

363. 팬들을 위해 열심히 해주세요!
Please do your very best for the fans!

364. 빠른 시일내에 다시 보고 싶어요.
I hope to see you again in the near future.

365. 너무 오래 기다리지 않았으면 좋겠어요.
I hope I wouldn't have to wait too long.

366. 자주 앨범 내 주세요.
Please release albums more often.

367. (뮤직비디오/노래) 더 많이 만들어주세요.
Please make more music video/songs.

368. (   )와 콜라보 해주세요!
Please do a collaborative work with (   )!

369. (TV show name) 에 나와주세요!
Please be on (TV show name)

370. 사진 보내주세요!
Please send me a photo!

371. 싸인 해주세요!
Please give me your autograph!

372. 인증샷 찍어주세요!
Please make sure to take a proof shot!

373. 운동 열심히 하세요!
Please work out hard!

374. 기도 열심히 하세요!
Please pray hard!

375. 공부 열심히 하세요!
Please study hard!

376. 답장 해주세요!
Please write me back!

377. 제 선물 마음에 들었으면 좋겠어요!
I hope you like my gift!

378. 선물을 보면 제 생각을 해 주세요.
Please think of me when you look at my gift.

379. 제 편지 간직해주세요.
Please keep my letter!

380. 저를 잊지 말아주세요.
Don't forget me.

381.   (Kakao   ID/Instagram/Facebook)
알려주세요.
Please tell me your .(Kakao ID/Instagram/
Facebook).

382. 제 (Kakao ID/Instagram/Facebook) 은/는
(   ) 이에요.
(   ) is my (Kakao ID/Instagram/Facebook)

383. 친구 추가 해주세요.
Please add me as a friend.

384. 제 전화번호는 (   ) 이에요.
My phone number is (   ).

385. 전화해 주세요!
Please call me!

~ Useful Words ~

384. 선물 (gift)

385. 친구 (friend)

386. ~해주세요 (please do me ~sth)
Example) 노래 해주세요 (please sing me a song)

387. 편지 (letter / mail)

388. 언젠가는 (one day)

Closing statement

389. 사랑해요!
I love you! / We love you!

390. 항상 사랑해요!
I always love you! / We always love you!

391. 절대 잊지 않을게요!
I will never forget you! / We will never forget you!

392. 자주 방송에 나와주세요.
Please be on TV shows more often!

393. (TV쇼/콘서트/극장) 에서 볼게요!
I will see you at/on (TV show/concert/theater)

394. 행운을 빌어요.
Good luck to you.

395. 신의 가호가 있기를!
May the grace of God be with you!

396. 행운의 여신이 함께 하기를!
May the lady luck be with you!

397. 즐거운 여행 되세요!
Have a fun trip!

398. 다시 만날때까지.
Until we meet again.

399. 그때를 기다릴게요.
I will wait for that moment.

400. 어디에 있어도
Wherever you are

401. 언제, 어디서나
Whenever, wherever

402. 웃음을 잃지 말아요
Don't forget to smile

403. 또 편지 할게요.
I will write you again.

404. 기다려주세요!
Please wait for me!

405. 사라지지 말아요!
Don't disappear!

406. 얼굴 좀 자주 보여주세요.
Show us your face more often.

407. 항상 건강하세요.
Always be healthy.

408. 빨리 컴백하주세요!
I hope you make a comeback very soon!

409. 군대에서 돌아올때까지 기다릴게요.
I will wait until you come back from the army.

410. 시간은 금방 지나갈거에요.
Time will fly.

411. 인내심을 갖고 기다릴게요.
I will wait patiently.

412. 너무 바쁜 것 알아요.
I know you are very busy.

413. 답장 못해줘도 실망하지 않을거에요.
I won't be disappointed if you can't write me back.

414. 시간 내서 편지 읽어줘서 고마워요.
Thank you for taking the time to read my letter.

415. 행복하세요!
Be happy!

416. 잘 지내요!
Take care!

417. 보고싶을 거에요.
I will miss you.

418. (   )가
From (   )

~ Useful Words ~

419. 즐거운 (pleasant / joyful / entertaining)
Example) 즐거운 노래 (joyful song)

420. 자주 (often)

421. 또 (again)

422. ~할게요 (I will~)
Example) 노래 할게요 (I will sing a song)

Fan Mail
Templates &
Samples

(태양 오빠)에게,
Dear Taeyang oppa,

안녕하세요? 제 이름은 (안드레아) 에요. 저는 (브라질)에 살아요. 저는 (12)살 이에요.
Hi, how are you? My name is (Andrea). I live in (Brazil). I am (12) years old.

처음으로 (오빠)에게 편지를 써요. 한국어 잘 못하지만 이해해주세요. 하지만 최선을 다할거에요.
This is my first time writing a letter to (oppa=you). Please excuse my bad Korean. But I will do my best.

(오빠)의 노래를 들으면 눈물이나요. 데뷔때부터 팬이었어요. (오빠)의 (콘서트)에 갔었어요.
I cry when I hear/listen to (your) song. I've been a fan since debut. I went to (your) (concert).

(오빠)는 저에게 큰 영감이에요. 매일 (오빠)의 노래를 들어요. 정말 정말 행복해요.
(You) are a huge inspiration to me. I always listen to (your) song. I am really really happy.

언제나 훌륭한 (노래)에 감사하고 있어요. 모든 팬들이 고마워해요.
I am always grateful for your outstanding (song). All the fans are thankful for it.

또 편지 할게요. 항상 웃음을 잃지 마세요.
I will write you again soon. Please don't forget to smile.

(안드레아)가
From (Andrea)

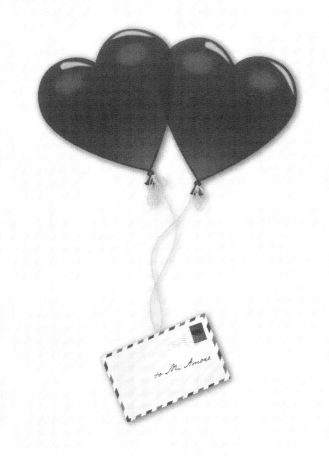

(아이유 언니)에게
Dear (IU unnie),

오랜만에 편지를 써요. 그동안 별일 없었어요?
(언니)에게 하고 싶은 이야기가 많아요.
It's been a while since I wrote to you. Anything new down your way? I have so many
things to share with (unnie=you).

(언니)의 뉴스를 보았어요. 저는 언제나 (언니)를
믿어요. 누가 뭐라고 하던지. 그런 소문따위 믿
지 않아요.
I saw the news about (you). I always trust
(you). Whatevery they say. I don't believe the
rumors.

많이 슬프겠어요. 안티는 무시하세요. 부러워서
그러는거에요.
You must be very sad. Just ignore anti fans.
They act like that because they are jealous.

건강이 가장 중요해요. (언니)의 행복이 (제)의
행복잉요.
Health is the most important thing. (Your)
happiness is (my) happiness.

(제)걱정은 하지 말아요.
Don't worry about (me).

또 편지 할게요.
I will write you again.

(지니)가
From (Jinny)

(앰버 씨)에게
Dear (Amber (formal),

안녕하세요? 제 이름은 (마이클)이에요. (알게되
어서) 기뻐요.
Hi, how are you? My name is (Michael). It's a
pleasure (knowing) you.

저는 (텍사스)에 살아요. 이곳은 (도시)에요. 제
별명은 (피카츄)에요.
I live in Texas. It is a city. My nickname is
Pikachu.

저는 (앰버 씨)에게 편지 쓰려고 한국어를 공부
해요.
I study Korean so I can write a letter to
(앰버 씨=you).

한국에 가보고 싶어요. 항상 보고싶어요.
I want to visit Korea. I always mis you.

당신과 같은 사람은 이 세상에 없어요. 덕분에
매일 행복해요.
There is no one like you in the world. Thanks
to you, I am happy everyday.

고마움에 보답할게요.
I will repay you for your kindness.

시간 내서 편지 읽어줘서 고마워요.
Thank you for taking the time to read my letter.

잘 지내요!
Take care!

(마이클)이
From (Michael)

(효린 누나)에게
Dear (Hyorin nuna),

해냈어요! 대상 타신것 축하해요! 그럴 자격이
있어요.You did it! Congratulations on winning
the daesang (grand prize)! You deserve it.

새 앨범에 있는 곡들 전부 다 좋아요. 최고중의
최고에요. 제 느낌은 틀린적이 없어요.
I like every single song in the album. You are
the best of the best. My feelings have never
been wrong.

너무 열심히 일하지 마세요. 파티 너무 많이 하
지 마세요. 음주운전은 절대 안되요!
Don't work too hard. Don't party too hard.
Drunk driving is never okay!

자주 앨범 내 주세요.
Please release albums more often.

또 편지 할게요.
I will write you again.

(타일러)가
From (Tyler)

(슈가 오빠)에게
Dear (Suga oppa),

그동안 별 일 없었어요? 정말 오랜만이에요!
It really has been a long time! Anything new
down your way?

(콘서트)**에서 (오빠)* 를 보았어요.
I saw (you)* at/in the (concert)**.

(오빠) 가 나와 같은 하늘 아래에 살고 있다는 사
실에 기분이 너무좋아요.
The fact that (oppa=you) and I live under the
same sky (in the same world) makes me feel
so happy.

고맙다는 표현을 어떻게 해야 충분한지 모르겠
어요. 부끄러움을 좀 타지만, 고마워요.
I don't know how to thank you enough. I am a
little shy to say this, but thank you.

이 세상에 단 하나뿐인 존재가 되어줘서 고마워
요.
Thank you for being the one and only.

군대에서 돌아올때까지 기다릴게요.

I will wait until you come back from the army.

(해나)가
From (Hannah)

사랑하는 (이특 오빠)에게
To my dearest (Lee Teuk oppa),

생일 축하합니다!
Happy Birthday!

(오빠) 는 하늘이 주신 선물이에요. (오빠)는 세상에 단 하나밖에 없는 사람이에요.
(Oppa=you) are a gift from heaven. You are the one and only person in the world.

술 너무 많이 마시지 마세요. 몸에 좋은 것 많이 먹어요.
Don't drink too much. Eat lots of things that are good for your body.

(오빠) 행복이 (저)의 행복이에요! (오빠) 가 항상 제 곁에 있어주었으면 좋겠어요.
(Your) happiness is (my) happiness! I always want to have (you) right here by my side.

팬들을 위해 열심히 해주세요!
Please do your very best for the fans!

제 선물 마음에 들었으면 좋겠어요!
I hope you like my gift!

선물을 보면 제 생각을 해 주세요.
Please think of me when you look at my gift.

행운의 여신이 함께 하기를!
May the lady luck be with you!

시간 내서 편지 읽어줘서 고마워요.
Thank you for taking the time to read my
letter.

행복하세요!
Be happy!

(신디아) 가
From (Cynthia)

사랑하는 (현아 누나)에게
To my dearest (Hyuna noona),

잘 지냈어요? 오랜만에 편지를 써요.
How have you been? It's been a while since I wrote to you.

(사인회)** 에서 (누나)* 를 보았어요. 모두에게 친절해서 좋아요.
I saw (nuna=you)* at the (fan signing)**. I like the fact that you are kind to everyone.

몸매가 정말 좋으세요. 어떻게 몸매를 유지해요? 정말 완벽해요. 언제부터 그렇게 (예뻤어요)?
You are in such great shape. How do you stay in shape? You are really perfect. Since when have you been so (pretty)?

모든걸 다 가진 사람이에요. 훌륭한 아내가 될거에요.
You are a man who has everything. You will make a great wife.

(누나) 를 사랑하는 팬들이 정말 많아요.
There are many fans who love (you).

(우리)가 (콘서트)에 응원하러 갈거에요.
We will be at the (concert) to support you.

큰 소리로 외칠거에요.I will cry at the top of
my voice.

함께 노래 할거에요. 형광봉을 흔들거에요.
I will sing along with you. I will be waving a
light stick.

팬들을 위해 열심히 해주세요!
Please do your very best for the fans!

신의 가호가 있기를!
May the grace of God be with you!

잘 지내요!
Take care!

(카를로스)가
From Carlos

~ Useful Conjunction / Transition Words ~

그리고 – And 그러나 – But 하지만 – However

무엇보다 – Above all 그래도 – Nevertheless

아참! – Oh! (When something suddenly comes to your mind)

그래서 – As a result 물론 – Of course

아쉽게도 – Regrettably 사실 – In fact

그렇기는 하지만 – Even so

우습게도 – Funny enough

제 생각에는 – In my opinion

특이하게도 – Strangely enough

믿기 어렵지만 – Although it's hard to believe

불행하게도 – Unfortunately

How to Write
Common
Names in
Hangul
Korean Alphabet

Abel – 아벨	Amos – 아모스
Abigail – 아비가일	Amy – 에이미
Abraham – 에이브러햄	Anais – 아나이스
Ace – 에이스	Andra – 안드라
Ada – 아다	Andrea – 안드레아
Adam – 아담	Andrew – 앤드류
Adela – 아델	Andy – 앤디
Adelio – 아델리오	Angel – 엔젤
Adolph – 아돌프	Angela – 앤젤러
Adonis – 아도니스	Angelica – 안젤리카
Adora – 아도라	Anika – 애니카
Agatha – 아가타	Anna – 안나
Aggie – 애기	Annie – 애니
Agnes – 아그네스	Anthony – 안토니
Aida – 아이다	Apollo – 아폴로
Aileen – 에일린	Aria – 아리아
Ailish – 앨리쉬	Ariel – 아리엘
Aimee – 에이미	Arista – 아리스타
Alan, Allan – 앨런	Arnold – 아놀드
Albert – 앨버트	Aaron – 아론
Albino – 앨비노	Arthur – 아서
Alex – 알렉스	Arvid – 아비드
Alexa – 알렉사	Asha – 아샤
Alexis – 알렉시스	Ashley – 애슐리
Alexandra – 알렉산드라	Aster – 아스터
Alexandria – 알렉산드리아	Astin – 아스틴
Alexander – 알렉산더	Aurora – 오로라
Alfred – 알프레드	Austin – 오스틴
Ali – 알리	Autumn – 오텀
Alice – 앨리스	Ava – 아바
Alicia – 앨리샤	Baba – 바바
Alika – 앨리카	Bailey – 베일리
Allie – 앨리	Bambi – 밤비
Allison – 앨리슨	Barbara – 바바라
Aloha – 알로하	Barbie – 바비
Alvin – 앨빈	Barley – 발리
Alyssa – 앨리사	Barney – 바니
Amanda – 아만다	Baron – 바론
Amber – 앰버	Basil – 배즐
Ami – 아미	Baxter – 백스터

Beatrice – 비아트리스	Caleb – 케일럽
Beau – 보우	Caley – 캘리
Bebe – 베베	Calix – 캘릭스
Beck – 벡	Calla – 칼라
Becky – 베키	Callia – 칼리아
Belita – 벨리타	Cameron – 카메론
Bella – 벨라	Camilla – 카밀라
Belle – 벨	Captain – 캡틴
Benecia – 베네치아	Cara – 카라
Benedict – 베네딕트	Carmel – 카멜
Benny – 베니	Carmen – 카르멘
Benjamin – 벤자민	Caroline – 캐롤라인
Berg – 버그	Carlos – 카를로스
Bessie – 베시	Cassandra – 카산드라
Biana – 비안나	Casey – 캐시
Bianca – 비앙카	Cassidy – 캐시디
Bibiane – 비비안	Catherine – 캐서린
Billy – 빌리	Cecil – 세실
Bingo – 빙고	Celestyn – 셀레스틴
Bishop – 비숍	Celina – 셀리나
Bliss – 블리스	Cha Cha – 샤샤
Blondie – 블론디	Chloe – 클로에
Bonita – 보니타	Champ – 챔프
Bono – 보노	Charles – 찰스
Boris – 보리스	Charlie – 찰리
Boss – 보스	Chase – 체이스
Brainna – 브래나	Chavi – 샤비
Brandon – 브랜든	Chelsea – 첼시
Breanna – 브리나	Cherie – 쉐리
Brian – 브라이언	Chloe – 클로에
Briana – 브리아나	Chrissy – 크리시
Bridget – 브리지트	Christian – 크리스챤
Bright – 브라이트	Christina – 크리스티나
Brittany – 브리태니	Christopher – 크리스토퍼
Brooke – 브루크	Cindy – 신디
Bruno – 브루노	Clara – 클라라
Buck – 벅	Clark – 클락
Buddy – 버디	Claude – 클라우드
Bunny – 버니	Claudia– 클라우디아
Caesar – 시저	Cleo – 클레오

Cleta – 클레타
Coco – 코코
Cody – 코디
Colin – 콜린
Connie – 코니
Conrad – 콘라드
Corby – 코비
Crystal – 크리스탈
Courtney – 코트니
Cyclone – 사이클론
Cyma – 시마
Daina – 데이나
Daisy – 데이지
Dali – 달리
Daniel – 다니엘
Danielle – 다니엘레
Danika – 다니카
Darby – 다비
Daria – 다리아
Darin – 다린
Dario – 다리오
Darwin – 다윈
Dave – 데이브
David – 다비드
Dean – 딘
Della – 델라
Delling – 델링
Delphine – 델핀
Dennis – 데니스
Derry – 데리
Destiny – 데스티니
Deva – 데바
Dexter – 덱스터
Diallo – 디알로
Dick – 딕
Dino – 디노
Dixie – 딕시
Donald – 도널드
Donna – 돈나
Doris – 도리스

Dorothy – 도로시
Douglas – 더글라스
Duke – 듀크
Duncan – 던컨
Dustin – 더스틴
Dylan, Dillon – 딜런
Dyllis – 딜리스
Eavan – 에반
Ebony – 에보니
Edan – 에단
Edeline – 에델린
Eden – 에덴
Edgar – 에드가
Edith – 에디스
Edmund – 에드문드
Edward – 에드워드
Edwin – 에드윈
Eilis – 엘리스
Eldora – 엘도라
Elin – 엘린
Elisha – 엘리샤
Elizabeth – 엘리자베스
Elle – 엘르
Elroy – 엘로이
Elsa – 엘사
Elvis – 엘비스
Elysia – 엘리시아
Emilie, Emily – 에밀리
Emery – 에머리
Emma – 엠마
Enoch – 에녹
Eric – 에릭
Erica – 에리카
Erin – 에린
Eris – 에리스
Esteban – 에스테반
Esther – 에스더
Ethan – 에단
Eugene – 유진
Eva – 에바

Evan – 에반
Eve – 이브
Evelyn – 이벨린
Farrell – 파렐
Favian – 파비앙
Fedora – 페도라
Ferdianand – 퍼디난드
Felice – 펠리체
Felix – 펠릭스
Fella – 펠라
Fidelio – 피델리오
Filia – 필리아
Fleta – 플레타
Florence – 플로렌스
Floria – 플로리아
Forrest – 포레스트
Frederick – 프레데릭
Freeman – 프리맨
Frances – 프란시스
Gabriel – 가브리엘
Gabriella – 가브리엘라
Gemma – 젬마
Geoffrey – 제프리
George – 조지
Gilbert – 길버트
Gili – 길리
Giovanni – 지오반니
Gloria – 글로리아
Goofy – 구피
Grace – 그레이스
Grania – 그라니아
Gregory – 그레고리
Hailey – 헤일리
Haley – 할리
Halona – 할로나
Hannah – 한나
Happy – 해피
Harace – 헤레이스
Harley – 할리

Harold – 해럴드
Harry – 해리
Heba – 헤바
Helen – 헬렌
Helia – 헬리아
Henry – 헨리
Hera – 헤라
Hubert – 휴버트
Huey – 휴이
Hugh – 휴
Humphery – 험프리
Hunter – 헌터
Ian – 이안
Iliana – 일리아나
Indira – 인디라
Ingrid – 잉그리드
Irene – 아이린
Irina – 아이리나
Iris – 아이리스
Isaac, Issac – 아이작
Isabel – 이사벨
Isadora – 이사도라
Jace – 제이스
Jack – 잭
Jackson – 잭슨
Jacob – 제이콥
Jaclyn – 재클린
Jade – 제이드
James – 제임스
Jane – 제인
Jasmine – 쟈스민
Jason – 제이슨
Jasper – 제스퍼
Jefferson – 제퍼슨
Jeffrey – 제프리
Jenna – 제나
Jennifer – 제니퍼
Jennie- 제니
Jeremy – 제레미
Jericho – 제리코

Jerome - 제롬
Jerry - 제리
Jess - 제스
Jessica - 제시카
Jessie - 제시
Jesus - 헤수스 (Spanish)
Jodie - 조디
Johanna - 조안나
John - 존
Jolly - 졸리
Jonathan - 조나단
Jordan - 조단
Joseph - 조셉
Joshua - 죠수아
Joy - 조이
Jud - 쥬드
Judith - 쥬디스
Julia - 쥴리아
Juliana - 쥴리아나
Juliet - 쥴리엣
Justin - 져스틴
Kali - 칼리
Kara - 카라
Karena - 카레나
Karis - 카리스
Kassia - 카시아
Kate - 케이트
Katherine, Kathryn - 케서린
Kathy - 케티
Katie - 케이티
Kaitlyn - 케이슬린
Kayla - 카일라
Kaylee - 카일리
Kellan - 켈란
Kelley - 켈리
Kelsey - 켈시
Kenneth - 케네스
Kerri - 케리
Kevin - 케빈
Kiara - 키아라

Kimberly - 킴벌리
Klaus - 클라우스
Kori - 코리
Kuper - 쿠퍼
Kyle - 카일
Kylie - 카일
Kyra - 키라
Lakia - 라키아
Lala - 랄라
Lamis - 라미스
Lani - 라니
Lappy - 래피
Lara - 라라
Laura - 로라
Lauren - 로렌
Lavina - 라비나
Lawrence - 로렌스
Lee - 리
Leena - 리나
Lelia - 렐리아
Leo - 레오
Leonard - 레오나드
Leopold - 레오폴드
Leslie - 레슬리
Lev - 레브
Lewis, Louis, Luis - 루이스
Lidia - 리디아
Lily - 릴리
Lina - 리나
Linda - 린다
Lisa - 리사
Lloyd - 로이드
Lonnie - 로니
Lottie - 로티
Louis - 루이스
Lowell - 로웰
Lucia - 루시아
Lucifer - 루시퍼
Lucy - 루시

Lukas – 루카스	Morris – 모리스
Luna – 루나	Murphy – 머피
Mabel – 마벨	Nadia – 나디아
Mackenzie – 맥킨지	Nami – 나미
Madeline – 마들린	Nana – 나나
Madison – 메디슨	Nani – 나니
Madonna – 마돈나	Naomi – 나오미
Maggie – 매기	Nara – 나라
Makaio – 마카이오	Narcisse – 나르시스
Makayla – 마케이라	Natalie – 나탈리
Malissa – 맬리사	Nathan – 네이탄
Malo – 말로	Navid – 나비드
Mana – 마나	Neal – 닐
Mandelina – 만델리나	Neema – 니마
Manon – 마농	Nero – 네로
Marcia – 마르샤	Nia – 니아
Margaret – 마가레트	Nicholas – 니콜라스
Maria – 마리아	Nicole – 니콜
Mariah – 마리아	Nicky – 닉키
Marissa – 마리사	Nina – 니나
Martha – 마사	Noah – 노아
Martin – 마틴	Noel – 노엘
Mary – 매리	Odelia – 오델리아
Mathilda – 마틸다	Olga – 올가
Matthew – 매튜	Olive – 올리브
Maya – 마야	Oliver – 올리버
Megan – 메건	Olivia – 올리비아
Melina – 멜리나	Oscar – 오스카
Melissa – 멜리사	Owen – 오웬
Meriel – 메리엘	Pablo – 파블로
Michael – 마이클	Paige – 페이지
Michelle – 미쉘	Paloma – 팔로마
Mickey – 미키	Pamela – 파멜라
Minnie – 미니	Patricia – 패트리샤
Miranda – 미란다	Patrick – 패트릭
Misty – 미스티	Paul – 폴
Molly – 몰리	Pavel – 파벨
Monet – 모네	Peggy – 페기
Monica – 모니카	Pello – 펠로
Morgan – 모건	Penda – 펜다

Peppi – 페피
Peter – 피터
Petra – 페트라
Phila – 필라
Phillip – 필립
Phyllis – 필리스
Pinky – 핑키
Pluto – 플루토
Poco – 포코
Polo – 폴로
Pooky – 푸키
Poppy – 포피
Primo – 프리모
Prince – 프린스
Princess – 프린세스
Puffy – 퍼피
Rachel – 레이첼
Rabia – 라비아
Raina – 레이나
Ralph – 랄프
Rania – 라니아
Ravi – 라비
Rebecca – 레베카
Redford – 레드포드
Reggie – 레지
Rei – 레이
Remy – 레미
Rex – 렉스
Richard – 리차드
Ricky – 리키
Riley – 라일리
Ringo – 링고
Rio – 리오
Risa – 리사
Robbie – 로비
Robert – 로버트
Robin – 로빈
Rocky – 록키
Roja – 로하

Roland – 롤랜드
Rollo – 롤로
Romeo – 로미오
Rosemary – 로즈마리
Rosie – 로지
Roxy – 록시
Roy – 로이
Ruby – 루비
Rudolph – 루돌프
Rudy – 루디
Ryan – 라이언
Sabastian – 세바스챤
Sabrina – 사브리나
Sally – 샐리
Salvatore – 살바토레
Sam – 샘
Samantha – 사만다
Samson – 샘슨
Samuel – 새뮤엘
Sandy – 샌디
Sarah – 사라
Sasha – 사샤
Savannah – 사바나
Scarlet – 스칼렛
Scoop – 스쿠프
Sebastian – 세바스챤
Selina – 셀리나
Selma – 셀마
Serena – 세레나
Shaina – 샤이나
Shasa – 샤사
Shelby – 셸비
Sheri – 쉐리
Sierra – 시에라
Silvester – 실베스터
Simon – 사이먼
Solomon – 솔로몬
Sonia – 쏘냐
Sonny – 써니
Sophia, Sophie – 소피아, 소피

Stephanie – 스테파니
Stella – 스텔라
Steven – 스티븐
Sunny – 써니
Syndey – 시드니
Sylvester – 실베스터
Sylvia – 실비아
Talia – 탈리아
Talli – 탈리
Tanesia – 타네시아
Tania – 타냐
Taylor, Tailor – 테일러
Ted – 테드
Tess – 테스
Theodore – 시오도어
Thomas – 토머스
Timothy – 티모시
Tomo – 토모
Trisha – 트리샤
Tyler – 타일러
Umberto – 움베르토
Valencia – 발렌시아
Vanessa – 바네사
Vera – 베라
Verdi – 베르디
Veronica – 베로니카
Victoria – 빅토리아
Vincent – 빈센트
Violet – 바이올렛
Vivian – 비비안
Waldo – 왈도
Walter – 월터
Wallace – 월러스
Wendy – 웬디
William – 윌리엄
Wily – 윌리
Winston – 윈스톤
Woody – 우디
Yuki – 유키
Zachary – 재커리

Zena – 제나
Zenia – 제니아
Zeppelin – 제플린

If your name is not listed, try

http://roman.cs.pusan.ac.kr

You can type your English name and it will convert it into Korean Hangul.

Please check out other best sellers

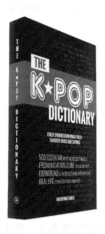

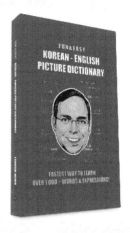

SUPER 500 KPOP Trivia Quiz Book
: 500 Fun-Filled Questions About
Your Favorite Idol

The biggest KPOP Trivia Book in the
world!

THE KPOP DICTIONARY:
Understand What Your
Favorite Idols Are Saying

FUN & EASY KOREAN-ENGLISH
PICTURE DICTIONARY:
The Easiest Way to Learn Over
1,000 Words & Expressions

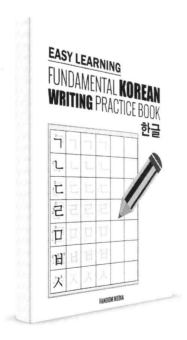

New Release
EASY LEARNING FUNDAMENTAL
KOREAN WRITING PRACTICE BOOK

Made in the USA
Columbia, SC
22 March 2020